Ephemeral

Shivangi Khanna

BookLeaf Publishing

India | USA | UK

Presentation by *BookLeaf Publishing*

Web: www.bookleafpub.com

E-mail: info@bookleafpub.com

ISBN: 9789363310384

First edition 2024

To all my loved ones, who have supported in every one of my endeavors, including becoming an anonymous poet.

ACKNOWLEDGEMENT

I would like to acknowledge the BookLeaf Publishing team for organizing #TheWriteAngle Writing Challenge and giving me this opportunity.

PREFACE

This journey began years ago, when I was only a reader. Here, I present to you my work as a writer, compiling my wonderings of the past several years. Life has thrown curveballs that nobody could have imagined, but they sparked my creative intuition and brought me to where I am today. I share my thoughts in the hope that every reader might connect with at least one word in this book, and hold that meaning close to their heart. Enjoy reading!

Beckoned

It's not tears I've shed, but fluid threads of pain,
Hidden from everyone's view.
The rhythm in my chest is slowing,
And life has conspired to stop me
From moving on,
From living.
Unseeing were my eyes
As for the last time,
The darkness sunk in
And it drowned me in itself.
Not bound by permission, my eyes opened
And light greeted me.
Inviting me to join
But never letting my chase end.
I surrendered to defeat, letting my head fall,
To find that I was the beckoning light.

Enough

2

The one my heart wants,
that it prays to be with,
has shattered.
To unite the pieces
will my courage be enough?

Wajood

3

What starts with love,
and end with it?
Your existence
in my life.

Unburdened

It was raining when you left
And I drowned myself as the heavens wept
Relieved that you finally set me free

Horizon

5

She was day and he was night
They needed each other
But could never meet one another
And so it went on
For eternity

Together

Place your hand in mine
And match your steps with me
Not only was it meant to be
But maybe our meeting is a necessity

Tea-ranny

When you have a headache
Make yourself a cup of chai
Then enjoy your break
And let your 'dil' go 'haaye'

Bittersweet

Your broken words seem like stories
Your adorable smiles- they're my life's lease
I think of the day you'll walk your own path
But will I be able to face that wrath?

Letters

You might be confused
If I say you're the cursive in my life.
But rest assured,
It's the greatest of compliments.
When the mind is prepared,
The hands print clearly,
The letters precisely formed.
But in the blink of an eye,
I am blindsided
By the deepening drawl
With the letters extended.
When two people meet,
The start is stuttered
But they awkwardly rub along
Until a rhythm is settled.
And like that, my hand,
My letters fumbled.
Tiptoeing closer
Until they connected.
You are the flowing cursive
That has me unconsciously snared,
Pulling me towards it
No matter how and where I've started.

Dreams

Be the person that gives you peace.
Do the work that tires your soul,
Angers your heart, and exhausts the mind.
But a laugh still whispers out,
The moment before you succumb
To a world stitched of dreams.

Chosen

Everyone says love is selfless
But sometimes, maybe love should be selfish
Perhaps, choose the one who loves you
Rather than the one you love

Twice shy

The trust I gave
Was returned by betrayal.
Now I need to trust myself,
But I haven't the courage.

If only

If only
This moment would linger
So I could confess
The secrets of my heart

Fortitude

You caught my eye
Standing proud in green
One amongst the hundreds of shriveled
Adorned by the jewels of winter
You caught my eye
A lone dandelion
Surrounded by winter frost
Decorated in frozen dew
You caught my eye
Encouraging me
To be like you

Heaven

Your journey with me was only 'till here,
Surpassing me in bounds.
I began to fly, without reason,
And my destination became heaven.

Puzzle

16

A conundrum, this life,
Leaving us intoxicated for more

Luck

17

One in millions will have such a destiny
To fall in love with this land of bounty
Where the wind chases the air
And the water laughs while I stare
Branches bow lazily, dipping their leaves
In the splashing water meeting the breeze

Morse

I don't understand the words of rain.
Each drop, tapping out
An indecipherable morse code
On my blurred windowpanes.
My heartbeat seems to, aligning
To the rhythm of nature's language,
Guiding me down memory lane.

Envy

Oh, but listen
To beauty's jealousy
That our pair
Is ruining her trade

Lantern wishes

Do you see all the floating wishes?
Flickering like will o'wisps?
It's time for the stars to descend
And light the floating lanterns.

The End

It told me to give up;
It said I wouldn't make it,
Warned me to let go.
There's no road to rocky,
Or ice cream even,
For me to fall astray.
I'll chart the path not taken,
Traverse the trail unmarked,
Check off the list
Of travelling metaphors,
While stepping on stones
Carved with taunts.
To come full circle,
And complete what I began.